Pianos

Music Makers

T H E   C H I L D ' S   W O R L D®,   I N C .

Pianos

Pamela K. Harris

THE CHILD'S WORLD®, INC.

Library of Congress Cataloging-in-Publication Data
Harris, Pamela K., 1962–
Pianos / by Pamela K. Harris.
p. cm.
Includes index.
Summary: Simple text describes parts of a piano
and how it is used to make music.
ISBN 1-56766-682-5 (lib. bdg. : alk. paper)
1. Piano—Juvenile literature. [1. Piano.] I. Title.
ML650 .H28 2000
786.2'192'2—dc21   99-059950

Credits

Translation: Neil Carruthers,
University of Canterbury, Christchurch, New Zealand
Graphic design: Brad Clemmons

Photo Credits

© www.comstock.com: cover, 3, back cover
© K.D. Dittlinger: 10
© PhotoDisc: 19, 20, 23
© Stone/Andy Sacks: 6, 16; Ian Shaw: 9; Bob Krist: 12;
   Don Smetzer: 15

Table of Contents

Guess what? The piano has a secret. Do you know what the secret is? The piano has strings you can't see. Can you guess where the strings are? They are inside the piano! The piano belongs to a group of musical instruments called **stringed instruments**.

The Keyboard

The piano has a **keyboard** with black and white keys. Each of the keys is matched to one, two, or three strings. Each key is also attached to a tiny hammer inside the piano. When you push a key, the hammer bangs against the strings—just like hammering a nail! The struck string makes a sound. The sound you hear is called a **note**.

Each key on the piano makes one note. ➔
Playing the piano makes your fingers strong.

The strings of the piano are different sizes. How thick or thin a string is makes a difference in the piano's sound. Thick strings make low notes and thinner strings make higher notes.

You can also push more than one piano key at a time. Then the piano makes a sound that is a combination of notes. This sound is called a **chord**.

← It is easy to see the strings and hammers inside this old *upright* piano.

Why Is a Piano Made of Wood?

Most pianos are made of wood. The wood creates a **soundbox** with the strings inside of it. When a hammer hits a string, the string begins to **vibrate**, or move back and forth. The vibrating string makes the sound you hear. The piano's wood soundbox carries the sounds and makes them louder.

← This piano tuner is carefully checking these *grand pianos*.

The Pedals

When you sit at a piano, you will see **pedals** near the floor. By pressing the pedals with your feet, you can change the **volume** of sound from the piano. One pedal makes the music quieter. Another pedal makes the notes last longer.

Practice makes perfect! Playing the piano takes lots of concentration. →

Who Invented the Piano?

About 300 years ago, an Italian man named Cristofori invented the piano. He called his new instrument *pianoforte,* which means "quiet and loud" in Italian. Over time, people shortened the name to "piano."

← This piano builder is adjusting the hammers before they are put inside a piano.

The Shapes of Pianos

Pianos come in many shapes and sizes. Most pianos are **uprights**. The strings in uprights are stretched up and down instead of sideways. A *giraffe piano* is a special type of upright. It has a very high back, just like the neck of a giraffe. In some countries, you can find square pianos with very short legs. To play a piano like this, you sit on cushions on the ground.

Another type of piano is the **grand piano**. Grand pianos are large, wide, and flat. Musicians often play grand pianos for concerts. They are the biggest pianos of them all.

A grand piano like this one might be played in an orchestra.

Ludwig van Beethoven was a great musician who played the piano. At one concert, he hit the keys so hard that they broke! Beethoven was deaf, so he could not hear the music he played. Instead, he felt the vibrations from the piano. Maybe that is why he hit the keys so hard!

Wolfgang Amadeus Mozart was another famous musician. He began playing the piano when he was just a little boy. Mozart wrote music to be played on the piano. Beethoven's and Mozart's piano music is very beautiful. Musicians still play their music today.

← Many famous musicians played the piano when they were young.

Pianos and Music

People play all types of music on the piano. You can hear pianos in jazz, rock, and classical music. Sometimes, pianos are played with other instruments in a group or band. Other times, a musician plays a piano all by itself. Would you like to learn how to play the piano?

Other Instruments with a Keyboard

player piano

miniature piano

upright piano

harpsichord

organ

electronic piano

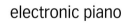

Glossary

chord (KORD)
Playing a chord is playing more than one note at a time. On a piano, pressing more than one key at a time plays a chord.

grand piano (GRAND pee-AN-oh)
A grand piano is the biggest type of piano. It is long, wide, and flat.

keyboard (KEE-bord)
The keyboard is the part of a piano that has black and white keys. Pressing down on the keys makes the piano play notes.

note (NOHT)
A note is a musical sound. Each key on a piano plays a different note.

pedals (PEH-dullz)
The pedals on a piano are levers near the floor. Pressing the pedals with your feet changes the piano's sound.

soundbox (SOUND BAHKS)
The soundbox is the body of a piano. It contains the strings and hammers and helps make the music louder.

stringed instruments (STRINGD IN-struh-ments)
Stringed instruments are musical instruments that use stretched strings to make their sounds. Pianos are stringed instruments.

uprights (UP-rites)
Upright pianos have high backs that are shaped like rectangles. Most pianos are uprights.

vibrate (VY-brayt)
When something vibrates, it moves back and forth. When the strings in a piano vibrate, they make sounds.

volume (VAHL-yoom)
Volume is how loud or quiet a sound is. To change a piano's volume, you press the keys harder or softer, or use the pedals.

24

Index